Piano · Vocal · Guitar

MELISSA ETHERIDGE
Lucky

ISBN 0-634-08451-8

HAL•LEONARD®
CORPORATION

7777 W. BLUEMOUND RD. P.O. BOX 13819 MILWAUKEE, WI 53213

In Australia Contact:
Hal Leonard Australia Pty. Ltd.
22 Taunton Drive P.O. Box 5130
Cheltenham East, 3192 Victoria, Australia
Email: ausadmin@halleonard.com

Visit Hal Leonard Online at
www.halleonard.com
www.melissaetheridge.com

MELISSA ETHERIDGE
Lucky

4   Lucky

11   This Moment

16   If You Want To

22   Breathe

28   Mercy

36   Secret Agent

44   Will You Still Love Me

50   Meet Me in the Dark

56   Tuesday Morning

64   Giant

71   Come On Out Tonight

78   Kiss Me

83   When You Find the One

LUCKY

Words and Music by
MELISSA ETHERIDGE

Moderately fast

I wan-na see___ how luck-y   luck-y can be,

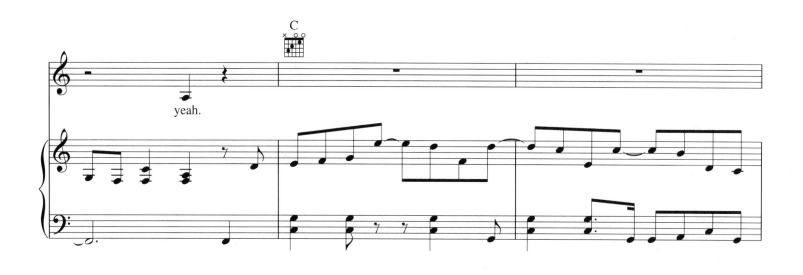

yeah.

THIS MOMENT

Words and Music by MELISSA ETHERIDGE
and JOHN SHANKS

with you.

With my hand on your skin, we can

slow - ly be - gin, I am free. Now the

IF YOU WANT TO

Words and Music by
MELISSA ETHERIDGE

BREATHE

Words and Music by RYAN JORDAN,
MARC WANNINGER, ANDREW DWIGGINS,
DOUGLAS RANDALL and BRANDON ARMSTRONG

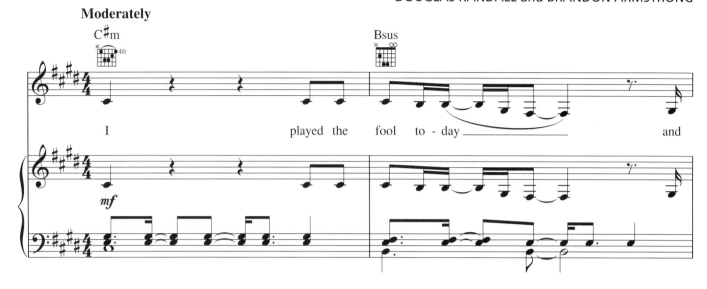

24

MERCY

Words and Music by MELISSA ETHERIDGE
and JONATHAN TAYLOR

SECRET AGENT

Words and Music by MELISSA ETHERIDGE
and JONATHAN TAYLOR

Heavy Rock

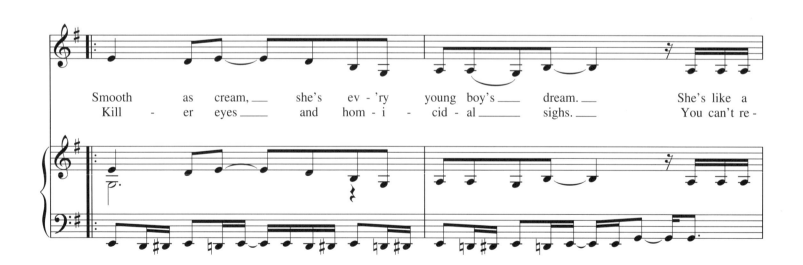

Smooth as cream, she's ev-'ry young boy's dream. She's like a
Kill - er eyes and hom-i - cid - al sighs. You can't re-

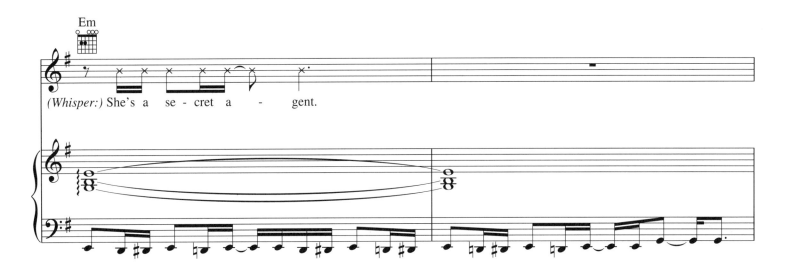

(Whisper:) She's a se - cret a - gent.

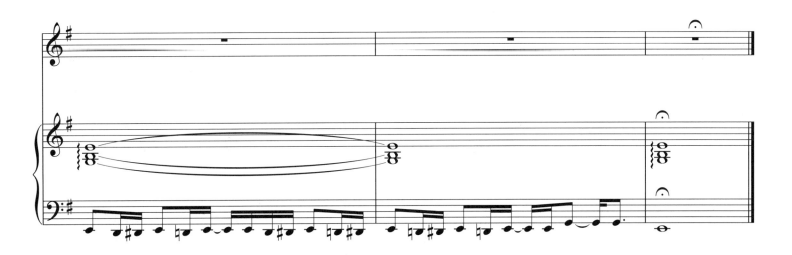

WILL YOU STILL LOVE ME

Words and Music by
MELISSA ETHERIDGE

46

MEET ME IN THE DARK

Words and Music by
MELISSA ETHERIDGE

Moderately slow

Keep your eyes _ down, keep your head _ low - ered, _ it
I know _ ev - 'ry - one has their un - spok - en fear, _ it

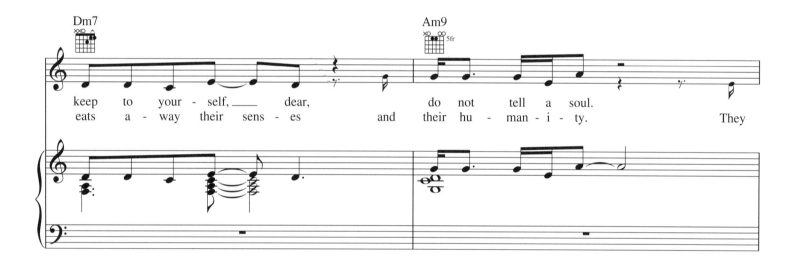

keep to your - self, _ dear, do not tell a soul.
eats a - way their sens - es and their hu - man - i - ty. They

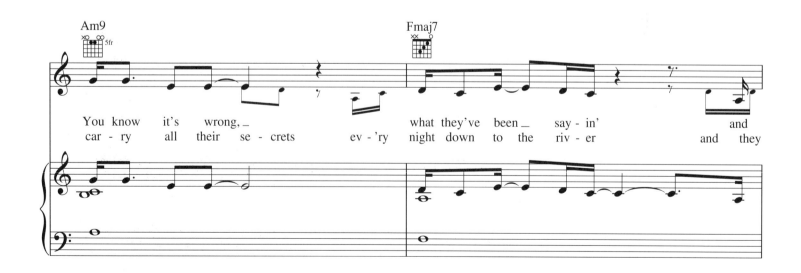

You know it's wrong, _ what they've been _ say - in' and
car - ry all their se - crets ev - 'ry night down to the riv - er and they

TUESDAY MORNING

Words and Music by MELISSA ETHERIDGE
and JONATHAN TAYLOR

Up and down_ this road I go, ___

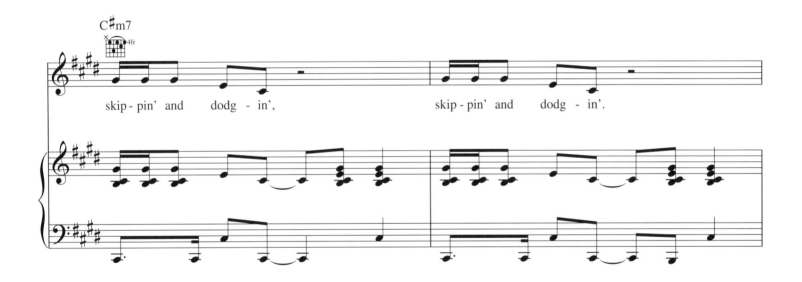

skip - pin' and dodg - in',　skip - pin' and dodg - in'.

Up and down_ this road I go, ___

GIANT

Words and Music by
MELISSA ETHERIDGE

COME ON OUT TONIGHT

Words and Music by
MELISSA ETHERIDGE

Moderately fast

Well, you got some tips ___ and you learned some licks, ___ you want to
good hard look ___ at this big star view, ___ don't be

try and teach this old dog ___ a new trick, huh?
bit - in' off more than you're ev - er gon - na chew, yeah.

Well, you told your friends ___ you'd have a lit - tle bit of fun, you want to
You can break the rules ___ when you play in the dark, but ev - 'ry

KISS ME

Words and Music by
MELISSA ETHERIDGE

Heavy Blues Rock

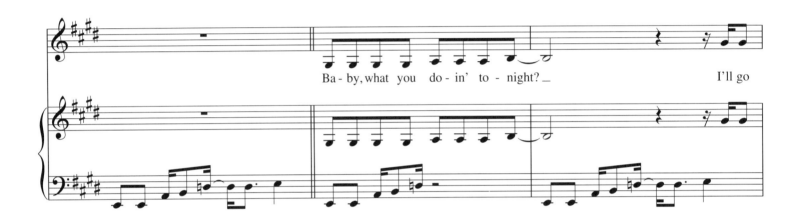

Ba - by, what you do - in' to - night? __ I'll go an - y-where that you wan - na go. __ I'll jump in my __ car, __ go

down to that __ bar, __ pre - tend I'm some-one that you don't know. __ I'll

what I've found ly - in' next to me.

Ba - by, what you do - in' to - night? I'll be an - y - one you want me to be,

just a girl in a bar, your per - son - al su - per - star. I just

WHEN YOU FIND THE ONE

Words and Music by
MELISSA ETHERIDGE

Moderately

I was a slick __ Mid - west - ern gal __ on the long __
say that I was cra - zy, I was that kind of girl. I had to

__ hard road __ in - to South - ern Cal. __ Did - n't find __
o - pen up a lot of oys - ters be - fore I found __ my - self __ a pearl. __ I had to

__ an - y crime, fill - in' up all my time, __ I had the dev - il in my bones __ and an
kiss a lot of frogs to find my grass was green e - nough, had to be face down in the gut - ter to see